To _____

From _____

On the occasion of _____

Date _____

CP

Text by Lois Rock
Copyright © 1993 Lion Publishing
Illustrations copyright © 1993 Claire Henley

The author asserts the moral right
to be identified as the author of this work

Published by
Lion Publishing
850 North Grove Avenue, Elgin, Illinois 60120, USA
ISBN 0 7459 2542 1

First edition 1993
10 9 8 7 6 5 4 3 2 1

Acknowledgments
The Lord's Prayer in its modern form as printed in *The Alternative Service Book 1980* is adapted from the version prepared by the International Consultation on English Texts (ICET) and is reproduced by permission of The Central Board of Finance of the Church of England.

Rock, Lois, 1953–
    The Lord's prayer for children / retold by Lois Rock: illustrated by Claire Henley
      ISBN 0-7459-2542-1 (hardback)
      ISBN 0-7459-2919-2 (paperback)
      1. Lord's prayer—Juvenile literature. I. Henley, Claire.
    II. Lord's prayer. III. Title.
    BV232.R63 1993   93-1412
    242'.722—dc20 CIP

Printed and bound in Singapore

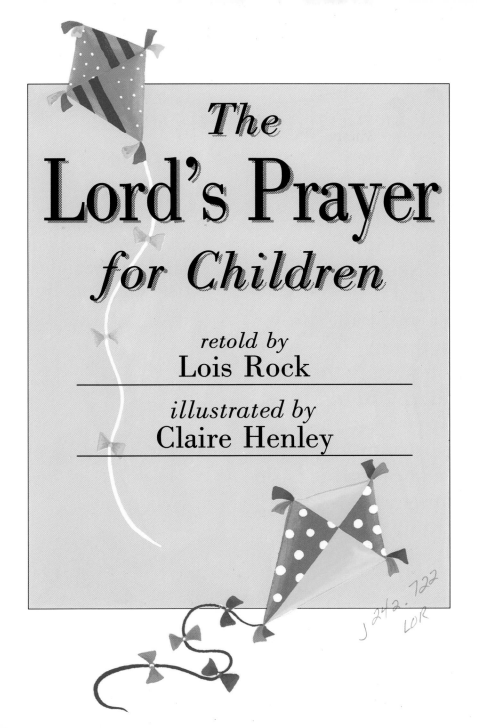

The Lord's Prayer
for Children

retold by
Lois Rock

illustrated by
Claire Henley

Our Father in heaven

Have you ever set out
to explore the world?
It seems so big,
and you seem so small.
You need a hug
to make you feel safe.
But just think:
God, who made the world,
is closer to you than the
wind on your face
and the air you breathe.
He loves you as his child
and wants you, and me,
to call him Daddy.

Dear God
You are a loving father
and you want us
to be your children.

Hallowed be your name

It's hard to imagine
what God must be like.
He made the whole world,
the sun and the sky,
the land and the sea,
the animals and the plants,
all the people—
and you.
It's a wonderful world
and God loves it
and takes care of it
all the time.

Dear God
I want everyone to
know how great and
good you are.

Your kingdom come

Some days begin
full of hope.
But many times, it seems
that things go wrong:
the world seems cruel,
and people are unkind.
If only they would do
as God wants,
let him be in charge,
then everything
would be better.

Dear God
I want the world to know
you are king.

Your will be done,
on earth as in heaven

If only creatures
didn't fight and kill.
If only spring came
without a wintertime.
If only people
were kind and loving.
If only they would listen
to you, dear God.
In heaven,
the Bible says,
everything is right
and good,
as you want it to be.

Dear God
I want the whole world
to live as you want.

Give us today our daily bread

Whatever we do,
dear God,
you still take care
of the world.
You send rain and sun
to make the plants grow,
so that animals and people
can have food
and everything they need
so they can be happy.

Dear God
Please give us food
and all we need
each day.

Forgive us our sins...

Whatever we do
we know that
you still want
to be friends with us.
You still want us
to call you father.

Dear God
Please forgive us when we
do wrong things.

...as we forgive those who sin against us

Why is it
that we get so angry
when other people
are unkind to us?
Deep inside,
we really want
to be friends.

Dear God
Help us to forgive those who
are unkind to us.

Lead us not into temptation...

Why is it
that we so often feel
it would be fun
to do something bad?

Dear God
Please stop us from wanting
to do bad things.

...but deliver us from evil

When things go wrong,
when something we like
gets broken or spoiled,
we get cross.
We want
to get our own back
on someone,
anyone.

Dear God
Please don't let the badness
in the world hurt us
or make us hit back.

For the kingdom, the power, and the glory are yours now and for ever. Amen

Sometimes,
when we feel sad,
we wonder
where you are.
But then we remember
how much you love us.
We find out
over and over again
that you are with us,
taking care of us
always.

Dear God
Help us to remember that
you made everything
and everyone;
that you are in charge
and always will be.

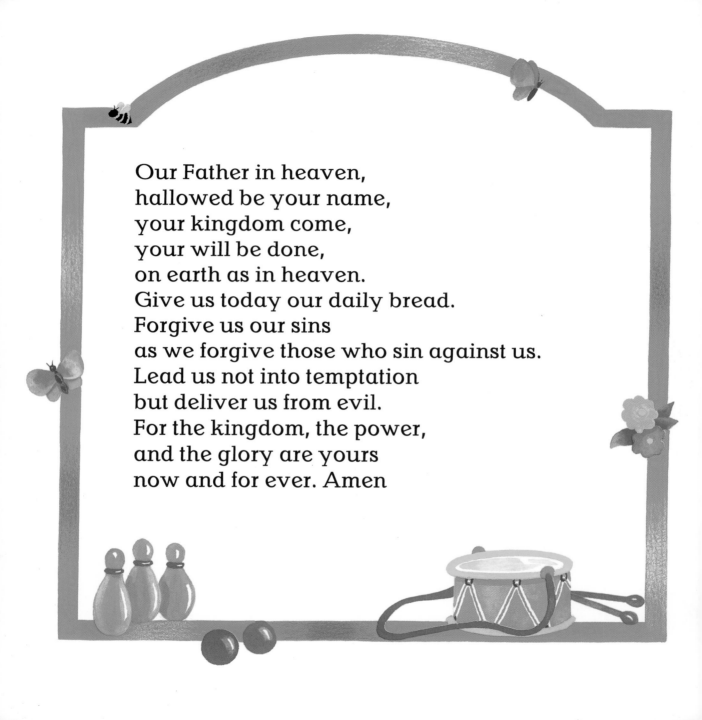

Our Father in heaven,
hallowed be your name,
your kingdom come,
your will be done,
on earth as in heaven.
Give us today our daily bread.
Forgive us our sins
as we forgive those who sin against us.
Lead us not into temptation
but deliver us from evil.
For the kingdom, the power,
and the glory are yours
now and for ever. Amen

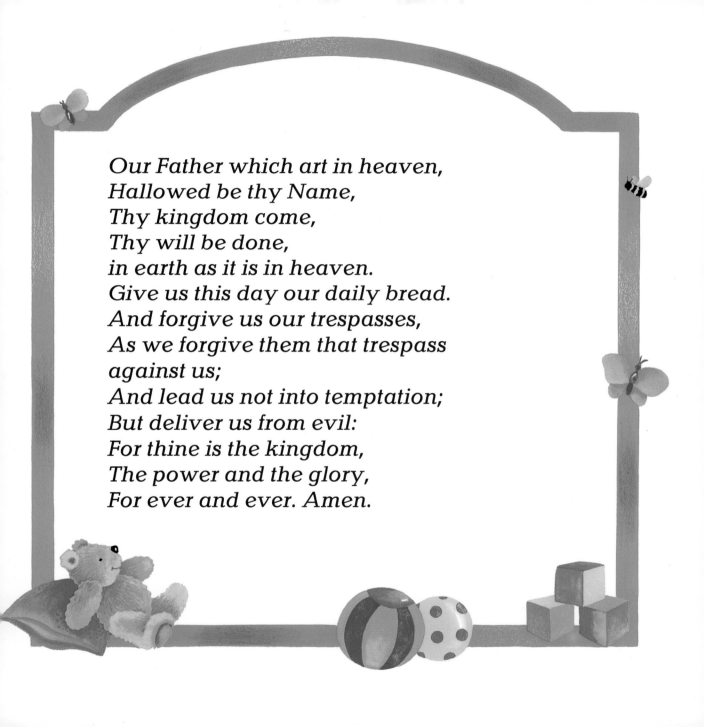

Our Father which art in heaven,
Hallowed be thy Name,
Thy kingdom come,
Thy will be done,
in earth as it is in heaven.
Give us this day our daily bread.
And forgive us our trespasses,
As we forgive them that trespass
against us;
And lead us not into temptation;
But deliver us from evil:
For thine is the kingdom,
The power and the glory,
For ever and ever. Amen.